MW01008927

THE FACE ON THE MILK CARTON

by
Caroline B. Cooney

Teacher Guide

Written by
Anne Troy
and
Mary Jane Gray

Note

The Laurel-Leaf paperback edition of the book published by Bantam Doubleday Dell was used to prepare this guide. The page references may differ in the hardcover or other paperback editions.

Please note: Please assess the appropriateness of this book for the age level and maturity of your students prior to reading and discussing it with your class.

ISBN 1-56137-729-5

To order, contact your local school supply store, or—

Novel Units, Inc.
P.O. Box 433
Bulverde, TX 78163-0433

Web site: www.educyberstor.com

Table of Contents

Skills and Strategies

Thinking
    Brainstorming, classifying
    and categorizing, comparing
    and contrasting

Comprehension
    Predicting, sequencing,
    cause/effect, inference

Writing
    Newspaper article, letter,
    comparison/contrast,
    narrative

Vocabulary
    Antonyms/synonyms,
    prefixes/suffixes

Listening/Speaking
    Participation in discussion,
    role play, interview

Literary Elements
    Character, setting, plot,
    flashback, conflict, figurative
    language, imagery, style,
    mood

Summary of *The Face on the Milk Carton*

This story centers around a strange situation faced by Janie, a fifteen-year-old girl. She is amazed and shocked when one day in the school cafeteria she sees the face of a missing child on her milk carton. She recognizes that this is a picture of her when she was younger. Janie struggles to understand how the parents she loves and considers her own could possibly have been involved in kidnapping her. Her search for an understanding of how this could be possible continues throughout the book. The reader is left at the end with a desire for more. Fortunately, there is a sequel which promises to fulfill this desire. The book should appeal to readers in grades 6-9.

About the Author

Caroline Cooney has written many books for young adults. Among these is *Whatever Happened to Janie?*, an ALA Best Book for Young Adults and the sequel to *The Face on the Milk Carton*. A second of her books, *Don't Blame the Music*, was also the recipient of this award. Mrs. Cooney lives in Connecticut and has three children.

Note:
It is not intended that everything presented in this guide be done. Please be selective, and use discretion when choosing the activities you will do with the unit. The choices that are made should be appropriate for your use and your group of students. A wide range of activities has been provided so that individuals as well as groups may benefit.

Introductory Activities and Information

Recommended Procedure:
Teachers are encouraged to adapt the Novel Unit to meet the needs of individual classes and students. You know your students best; we are offering you some tools for working with them. Here are some of the "nuts and bolts" for using these tools–a glossary of some of the terms used that will facilitate your use of this guide.

Bloom's Taxonomy: A classification system for various levels of thinking. Questions keyed to these levels may be:

- Comprehension questions, which ask one to state the meaning of what is written;
- Evaluation questions, which ask one to judge the accuracy of ideas;
- Synthesis questions, which ask one to develop a product by integrating the ideas in the text with the ideas of one's own.

Graphic Organizers: Visual representations of how ideas are related to each other. These "pictures," including Venn diagrams, the T-diagram, cluster circles, flow charts, attribute webs, etc., help students collect information, make interpretations, solve problems, devise plans, and become aware of how they think.

A variety of possible answers should be listed by the teacher, either on large sheets of paper or the chalk board. Only then should the students be asked to develop their own graphics. Students are encouraged to express their opinions, and to state what they know about a topic. The teacher lists these opinions and "facts" and later, as the students read and research, discovery may be made that some of their ideas are incorrect. These ideas may be crossed out on the sheets or the board. Students should be encouraged to elaborate on their answers, justify their opinions, prove their predictions, and relate what they have read to their own lives.

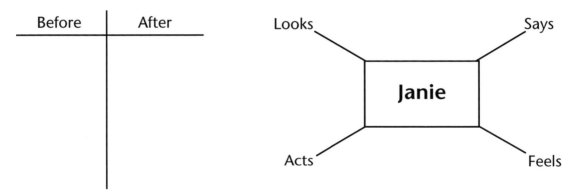

Cooperative Learning: Learning activities in which groups of two or more students collaborate. There is compelling research evidence that integration of social activities into the learning process–such as small group discussion, group editing, group art projects–often leads to richer, more long-lasting learning.

This book may be read one chapter at a time, using DRTA (Directed Reading Thinking Activity) Method. This technique involves reading a section, and predicting what will happen next by making good guesses based on what has already occurred in the story. The students continue to read and everyone verifies the prediction. (See pages 8-9 of this guide.)

Before reading, specific vocabulary words will be pointed out. Students may write simple definitions in their own words before reading. After reading, ask students to redefine the words referring to the context of the dictionary. Vocabulary Activities are also included.

After reading a chapter, brainstorm "what ifs." What if one or another character wasn't in the story, a character did something different, events followed a different sequence or didn't happen at all, etc. The teacher writes all these "what if" class responses on the board or a large sheet of paper. At the conclusion of the novel, the review of these "what ifs" may be used in writing a different development and/or ending for the novel.

Prereading Discussion Questions:

1. Importance of Mothers: What is the first memory you have of your mother? What are some of the things that only mothers do with their children? Do you remember getting angry with your mother when you were very young? Did you ever wander off at a store or mall? How did your mother react?

2. Older Parents: Are older parents more protective of their children, or less protective of them? How do they react to the child's friends? Are there any advantages of older parents? Disadvantages?

3. Teenage Problems: What are the most common ones? Relationship with parents? Friends? Opposite sex? School?

Initiating Activities:

Choose one or more of the following prereading activities to help students draw from their background of knowledge about the events and themes they will meet in *The Face on the Milk Carton*.

1. Prediction: Have the students examine the cover illustration and title. Ask what prediction they have about the book. Some prompts include: What can you tell me about the girl on the cover? How significant are the sandwich, apple, and hands on the cover? When and where and what do you think the cover of the book illustrates? Why are missing children's faces placed on milk cartons?

2. Anticipation Guide: Have students discuss whether they agree or disagree with the following statements and why. Have them reconsider these statements after reading the novel.

    a) Grandparents can take the place of parents.

    b) Confiding in friends can help (or hurt) you if you have a problem.

    c) If your parents do something to make you angry, you should talk to them about it.

    d) Once children are grown, their parents are no longer responsible for them.

    e) Crying when you're upset is healthy.

3. Brainstorming: Write the word "Kidnapped" at the center of a large piece of butcher paper or on the board. Have students say whatever comes to mind as you jot their ideas around the word. Help students "cluster" the ideas into categories. (See next page.)

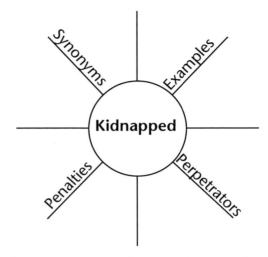

4. Log: Have students keep a response log* as they read.

*In one type of log, the student assumes the persona of one of the characters. Writing on one side of each piece of paper, the student writes in the first person ("I...") about his/her reactions to what happened in that chapter. A partner (or the teacher) responds to these writings on the other side of the paper, as if talking to the character.

*In the dual entry log, students jot down brief summaries and reactions to each section of the novel they have read. (The first entry could be based on a preview of the novel, for example, a glance at the cover and a flip through the book.)

Pages	Summary	Reactions
		These might begin:
		• *I like the part where...*
		• *This makes me think of the time...*
		• *Janie reminds me of (another character)*

Alternatively, students might simply jot responses on "sticky notes" for reference during discussions.

5. Prereading Vocabulary Activity:

a) Choose key vocabulary words from the story. Have students mark a chart to indicate whether they are unfamiliar with the word, have seen/heard it, or can define it. For example:

Word	No Idea	Have Seen/Heard	Can Define

b) Students then look up words they can't define. After discussing what the actions, setting, characters, problem and resolution are, have students fill out a chart in which they predict how the author will use the vocabulary words in the story.

The author will use the words to tell about:

<u>Setting</u>　　<u>Characters</u>　　　<u>Problem</u>　　　<u>Actions</u>　　　<u>Resolution</u>　　<u>Something Else</u>

6. *The Face on the Milk Carton* is an example of a realistic problem novel. In realistic fiction, characters are usually creations of the writer's imagination. The setting is real, usually a time and a place in the twentieth century. Help students fill in the chart comparing and contrasting historical fiction with realistic fiction.

	Realistic Fiction	**Historical Fiction**
Setting	Our world	Our world or earlier world
Characters	People like us	May or may not be people who lived at an earlier time
Action	Could happen	Could have happened, but not a true story
Problem	Could happen to us	Could have belonged to someone living at the time of the story
Examples	*Cracker Jackson*–Byars *Canyon Winter*–Morey *Dear Mr. Henshaw*–Cleary	*Johnny Tremain*–Forbes *Hiroshima*–Hersey *Lyddie*–Paterson

7. Story Map: Many stories have the same parts—a setting, a problem, a goal, and a series of events that lead to an ending or conclusion. These story elements may be placed on a story map, which helps a reader to understand and remember. (See page 10 of this guide.)

Using Predictions in the Novel Unit Approach

We all make predictions as we read—little guesses about what will happen next, how the conflict will be resolved, which details given by the author will be important to the plot, which details will help to fill in our sense of a character. Students should be encouraged to predict, to make sensible guesses. As students work on predictions, these discussion questions can be used to guide them: What are some of the ways to predict? What is the process of a sophisticated reader's thinking and predicting? What clues does an author give us to help us in making our predictions? Why are some predictions more likely than others?

A predicting chart is for students to record their predictions. As each subsequent chapter is discussed, you can review and correct previous predictions. This procedure serves to focus on predictions and to review the stories.

Use the facts and ideas the author gives.

Use your own knowledge.

Use new information that may cause you to change your mind.

Predictions:

_____

_____

_____

_____

_____

Prediction Chart

What characters have we met so far?	What is the conflict in the story?	What are your predictions?	Why did you make those predictions?

Story Map

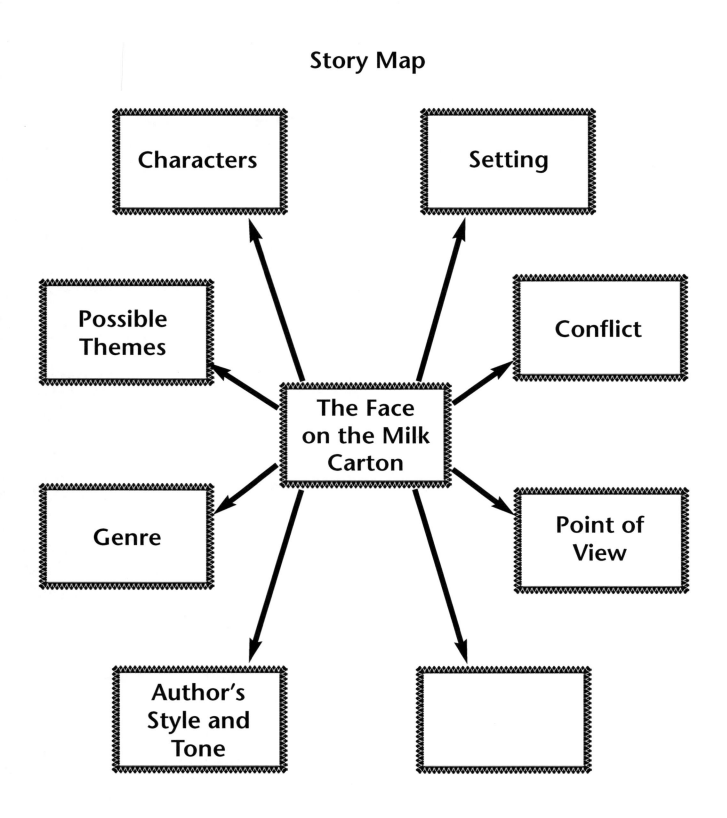

Characters

Setting

Possible Themes

Conflict

The Face on the Milk Carton

Genre

Point of View

Author's Style and Tone

Using Character Webs—In the Novel Unit Approach

Attribute Webs are simply a visual representation of a character from the novel. They provide a systematic way for the students to organize and recap the information they have about a particular character. Attribute webs may be used after reading the novel to recapitulate information about a particular character or completed gradually as information unfolds, done individually, or finished as a group project.

One type of character attribute web uses these divisions:

- How a character acts and feels. (How does the character feel in this picture? How would you feel if this happened to you? How do you think the character feels?)

- How a character looks. (Close your eyes and picture the character. Describe him to me.)

- Where a character lives. (Where and when does the character live?)

- How others feel about the character. (How does another specific character feel about our character?)

In group discussion about the student attribute webs and specific characters, the teacher can ask for backup proof from the novel. You can also include inferential thinking.

Attribute webs need not be confined to characters. They may also be used to organize information about a concept, object or place.

Attribute Web

The attribute web below is designed to help you gather clues the author provides about what a character is like. Fill in the blanks with words and phrases which tell how the character acts and looks, as well as what the character says and what others say about him or her.

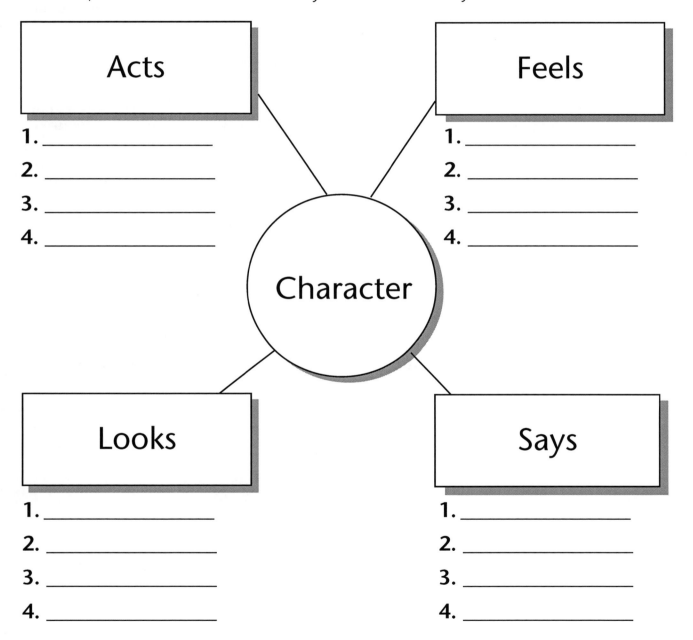

Acts

1. _____
2. _____
3. _____
4. _____

Feels

1. _____
2. _____
3. _____
4. _____

Character

Looks

1. _____
2. _____
3. _____
4. _____

Says

1. _____
2. _____
3. _____
4. _____

Attribute Web

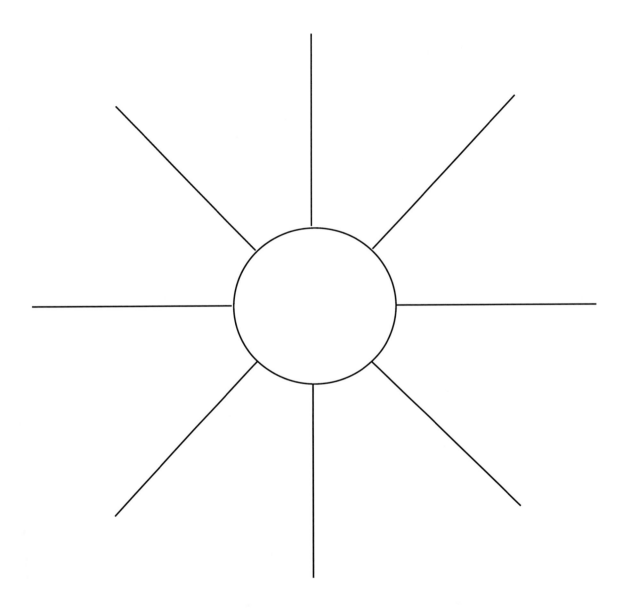

Chapter-by-Chapter Vocabulary, Discussion Questions, and Activities

Chapter 1: Pages 1-12
Chapter 2: Pages 13-23

Vocabulary:

fantasies 1	fabulous 2	chaotic 2	nauseating 4
filching 5	jaded 5	mortified 6	ruefully 7
anonymous 7	articulate 8	loathed 8	ransom 9
retrieved 11	deluge 15	resembled 17	wharves 17
marina 17	hydroplaned 19		

Vocabulary Activity:
Complete the following chart.

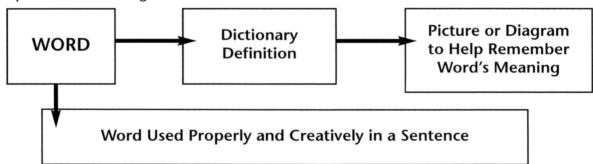

Discussion Questions and Activities:

1. What important event might have happened prior to the beginning of the story? *(Pages 11-12, Janie might have been kidnapped if it was really her picture on the milk carton.)*

2. What made Janie realize it was really her picture on the milk carton? *(Page 11, She remembered the dress and how it felt. She also remembered she had red braids.)*

3. Why didn't Janie's friends believe her when she said it was her picture? (page 11) How would you describe her friends? Are they like any of your friends?

4. How would you have answered Pete's comment that most of the children were not really kidnapped but taken by one parent after a divorce? (page 9) Could this be true? How could you check on this?

5. Janie's friend Reeve seemed to be a misfit in his family. What made him feel that way? (page 18)

6. Janie couldn't forget her face on the milk carton. (pages 21-22) What would you do in her place?

7. Janie said she had a perfectly normal family. What is a "perfectly normal family"? Brainstorm.

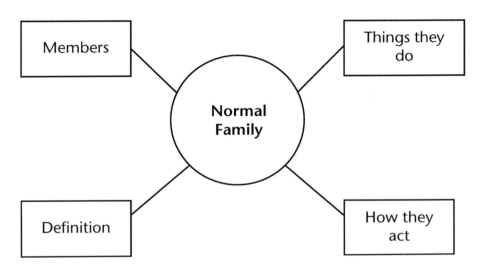

8. Using a T-diagram, begin a comparison of your family and Janie's.

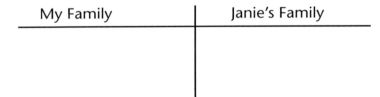

Prediction:
What will Janie do about the milk carton problem when she gets home? What will she ask her parents? How will she act?

Supplementary Activities:
1. Author's Craft—Characterization: Characterization is the way an author informs readers about what characters are like. **Direct characterization** is when the author describes the character. **Indirect characterization** is when the reader figures out what the character is like based on what the character thinks, says, or does.

   How would you use direct characterization to describe Janie? (fabulous red hair, only child, friendly, outgoing, etc.) How would you use indirect characterization to describe Janie? (Page 2, "She had gradually changed her name." Page 3, "She hated standing up in class. Hated hearing her voice all alone...")

2. Begin attribute webs for Janie and her parents. (See pages 11-13 of this guide.)

3. How many children are kidnapped each year? Who are the kidnappers? What are the penalties for kidnapping? Research.

4. Writing: This novel does not have chapter titles. A writer usually uses chapter titles to indicate something that might happen, or to create suspense to encourage the reader. After you read a chapter, write what you think would be the best chapter title. The teacher will post all titles and the class will vote for the best. The best chapter titles will be listed on the bulletin board.

Chapter 3: Pages 24-36
Chapter 4: Pages 37-46

Vocabulary:

tiara 25	ascending 26	immortalized 26	deranged 26
contours 28	rara avis 30	plummeted 30	decoupage 35
cuisines 35	prisms 37	sophomoric 38	sadist 39

Vocabulary Activity:
Words in Context: Ask students to "guess" at the meaning from context, telling why for each guess. Make a list of "why answers" to teach context clues.

Discussion Questions and Activities:
1. The word "daymare" is used in these chapters to explain what Janie was experiencing. What is a daymare? How does it differ from a nightmare? (page 38)

2. Janie's parents had many pictures of her, but no baby pictures. Why? *(Page 27, "Because they never got around to buying a camera till Janie was five.")* Why didn't Janie accept this now? Why do you think she never questioned this before?

3. Why did Janie run next door? *(Pages 28-29, She could not stand being in the empty house thinking.)* What did she learn about her past from Mrs. Shields? *(Page 30, She was a beautiful child about five years old when her very protective parents moved into the neighborhood.)*

4. Janie told her mother that she would need to get her birth certificate in order to apply for her driver's license. How did her mother react? *(Page 42, "It seemed to Janie that her mother's knuckles tightened and whitened.")* Could this be Janie's imagination?

5. Why didn't Janie share her fears with anyone?

6. What information did Janie remember in her "daymares"? Make a list of things that she had remembered. How much of this could have been just her imagination?

Prediction:
Janie has some serious emotions. How will she react to Reeve's playfulness and his friendship?

Supplementary Activities:
1. Literary Analysis—Flashback: Flashback involves the interruption of the action with a scene that occurred earlier, prior to the opening scene of the novel. Among the flashback devices are: recollections of the characters, narration by characters, dream sequences, and reveries. Complete the Flashback Chart on page 18 of this guide.

2. What is the earliest thing or happening that you can recall? Write a short paragraph describing the incident or thing.

3. Bulletin Board: Post pictures of students taken when they were three years old. Match current pictures with children's pictures.

Chapter 5: Pages 47-53
Chapter 6: Pages 54-62

Vocabulary:

hallucinations 52	perverted 53	frivolous 55	demented 56
sloths 59	catapulting 59	kidnapee 61	

Vocabulary Activities:
1. Identify the words with prefixes and suffixes. Find the root or base words.

2. Decide what other prefixes and suffixes may be added to vocabulary words and note how these change the word meanings. Make a new word list.

Discussion Questions and Activities:
1. Why do you think Reeve did not come back to Janie after the phone call? (page 48) Was he running away from Janie to forget the kiss? What other reasons might there be?

2. Why did Janie have trouble calling the 800 number? (pages 51-52) What could happen if Janie talked to the 800 number?

3. How do you think Janie was able to concentrate on driving or anything else when she was worried about the kidnapping? Was she able to act "normal" at the tailgate picnic? (pages 57-60)

Flashback Chart

Problems: There are flashbacks or suppressed memories and a story within a story in *The Face on the Milk Carton.* These are hard for students to understand without a time chart.

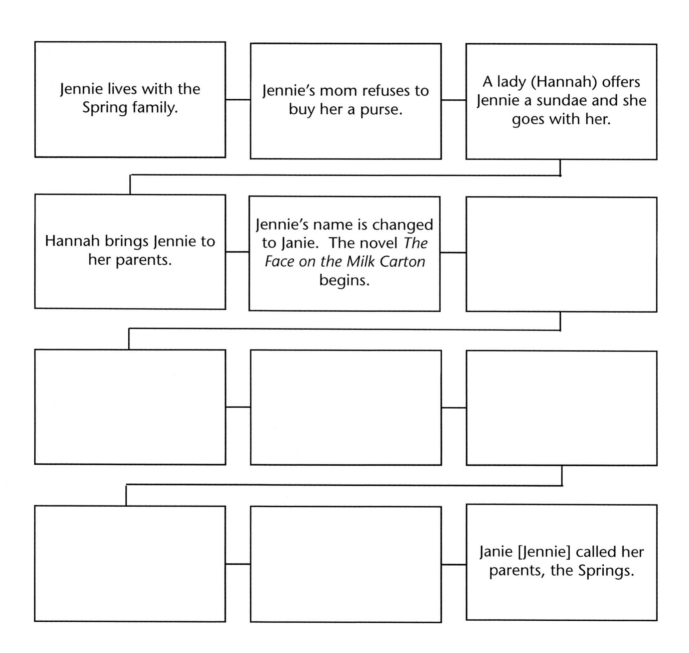

4. What attributes can you add to Janie's parents' web after the tailgating party and the practice drive with the car?

5. What is an "identity crisis"? (page 61) What was the teacher referring to in his comment on the paper? How did *identity crisis* really apply to Janie?

Prediction:
Jason did not remember Janie's picture episode on the milk carton, but what "terrible history" could Jane Johnson have?

Supplementary Activities:
1. Literary Analysis—Imagery: Imagery refers to words that appeal to the sense of sight, hearing, taste, touch, or smell. The author uses powerful words to help the reader see and feel. List these words on the Activity Sheet on page 20 of this guide.

2. Choose a section of dialogue. Complete the dialogue activity sheet on page 21 of this guide.

Chapter 7: Pages 63-68
Chapter 8: Pages 69-79

Vocabulary:

vague 63	extricate 64	reassurance 64	intact 64
aggressions 66	deprivation 69	tentatively 72	hostile 72
wended 77	preposterous 78		

Vocabulary Activity:
Students will make predictions about how the author will use the vocabulary words in regard to setting, characters, problem, action, etc.

Discussion Questions and Activities:
1. Why did Janie want to go through the safe deposit box? Why couldn't she do this? *(Page 64, She thought she might find something in it to help explain the confusion she felt about the kidnapping. She was undoubtedly hoping there would be something in the safe deposit box which would make things in her life all right again. It is highly possible, however, that she feared something in there would confirm her worst fears.)*

2. What did we learn about Janie's mother in this chapter? *(Pages 64-66, She was a highly organized lady who got rid of junk rather than just putting it in the attic. She had labeled the boxes in the attic.)*

Activity Sheet

The *setting* is the time and place where something happens. A writer describes the setting by telling about the sounds, sights, smells, tastes, and feelings of the place. As you read each chapter, fill in the chart by writing words and phrases from the story under each heading: see, hear, touch, taste, and smell.

See	Hear	Touch	Taste	Smell

Using Dialogue

Directions: Choose a bit of dialogue from the book to investigate. Fill in the chart to describe this way of writing and telling a story.

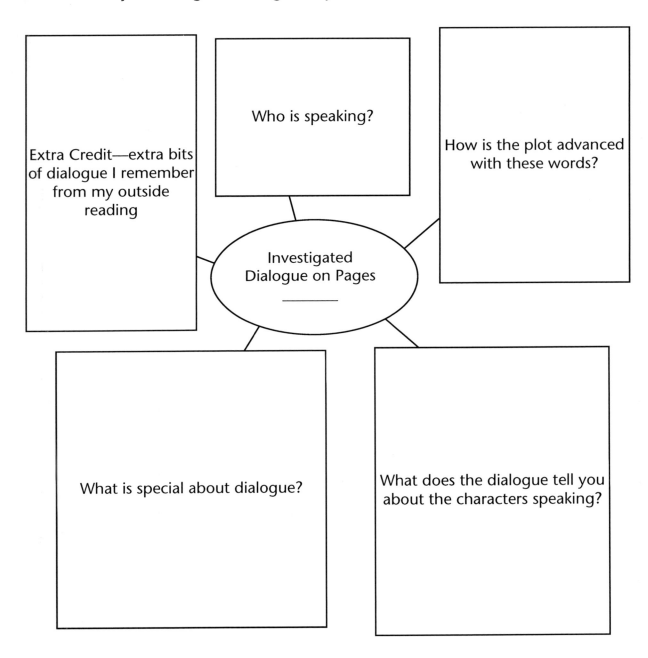

Extra Credit—extra bits of dialogue I remember from my outside reading

Who is speaking?

How is the plot advanced with these words?

Investigated Dialogue on Pages
_____

What is special about dialogue?

What does the dialogue tell you about the characters speaking?

3. What was mysterious about the old trunk? *(Page 67, It was cheap and locked, and it was labeled with the letter H.)* Why did Janie force the lock? What boring contents did she discover? *(page 68, old papers and pictures of a twelve or thirteen-year-old girl named Hannah)* What made the search worthwhile? *(Page 68, She found the dress pictured on the milk carton.)*

4. What did Janie suddenly remember about shopping? *(Pages 71-72, Her mother would not buy her a patent leather handbag, so she wandered off by herself in the mall. A lady with shiny hair bought her a sundae.)*

5. How did Janie really feel about her parents? Why did she have a hard time believing that they could have kidnapped her? *(Pages 70-71, "How could Mother and Daddy do it? Are they monsters?"; "He loves me, she thought. How could love arise from a crime like kidnapping?")*

6. A new boy, Dave, seemed to be interested in Janie, but she was not flattered by this. Why wasn't she thrilled with this attention? *(Page 76, She could think of nothing except the fact that she was really not who she thought she had been all her life.)*

7. What questions did Janie demand answers for? *(page 79, why there were no pictures of her until she was five, who Hannah was, and why her parents would not show her the birth certificate)*

Prediction:
Who do you think Hannah is?

Supplementary Activities:
1. Survey the stuff in your attic or basement. Are you a super-organized type? List the categories of "stuff" you find.

2. On what occasions must you have a birth certificate?

3. Literary Analysis—Conflict: Conflict is the struggle between two opposing forces, one of which is usually a person, often the main character, called the protagonist. Conflict occurs when the protagonist struggles against an antagonist or opposing force. The excitement in novels develops from the uses of conflict. Complete the Conflict Chart on page 24 of this guide as you read this novel.

4. Janie has many feelings of insecurity. Explore the term by completing an attribute web using your responses to these questions: What is the dictionary definition? What kind of situations promote insecurity? What are your feelings when insecure? Are there certain times of life that are filled with more insecurities? What are the best ways to handle insecurities? (See the next page of this guide.)

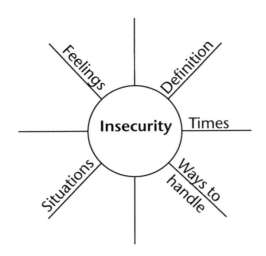

Feelings   Definition

Insecurity | Times

Situations   Ways to handle

Chapter 9: Pages 80-92
Chapter 10: Pages 93-99

Vocabulary:

assault 82	inequities 83	evoked 84	entice 86
docile 86	trauma 88	extricate 88	cyanide 95
clamored 95	ricocheting 95	authoritative 97	metallically 99

Vocabulary Activity:
Place the words for the days in categories. For example:

Descriptive	**Feelings**	**Actions**	**Things**
docile		extricate	cyanide

Discussion Questions and Activities:

1. Who was Hannah? *(Page 80, Mrs. Johnson told Janie that Hannah was her mother.)* Who were Mr. and Mrs. Johnson? *(page 80, Janie's grandparents)* What was Janie's reaction to this? *(Page 81, Janie felt a tremendous feeling of relief. She now thought she was Hannah's illegitimate daughter, rather than a kidnapee.)*

2. What did Janie learn about Hannah? *(Pages 83-84, She was an unusual child who did not fit in with the girls, who was involved in causes and eventually became involved with a cult, the Hare Krishna.)* Why do you think Hannah wanted to be involved in the cult?

3. How did the Johnsons try to be good parents to Hannah? *(Page 86, They tried everything to get her back–police, paying off the cult, debrainwashing her. Nothing worked.)*

The Nature of Conflict

As is true in real life, the characters in novels face many conflicts. When two people or forces struggle over the same thing, conflict occurs. The excitement in novels develops from the use of the three main types of conflict: (1) person against person; (2) person against nature or society; and (3) person against himself or herself.

Below list some of the conflicts from the novel. In the space provided, briefly describe the conflict and indicate which type of conflict is involved, writing "PP" for person vs. person, "PN" for person vs. nature or society, and "PS" for person vs. self. Then choose three of the conflicts and describe how each was resolved.

Conflict	Description	Type

Conflict #1 resolution: _____

Conflict #2 resolution: _____

Conflict #3 resolution: _____

4. When did the Johnsons first see Janie? *(page 87, when Hannah came home with Janie)*

5. Why did Hannah and the Johnsons fear the cult? *(Page 88, Hannah told them that the cult would try to get her and Janie back.)* How did Janie's parents react? *(Pages 88-89, They got the cooperation of IBM and they moved frequently, concealing their whereabouts.)*

6. Why do you think Hannah eventually left? What kind of hold did the cult have on her? Why did she leave Janie with her parents? *(Page 90, "She gave you up so you could have a real life...")* Why did the parents never write to Hannah or try to keep in contact with her? Why did they change their names?

7. What did Janie remember about a man with a red moustache? (page 90) Who could that have been?

8. When did Janie realize that her parents' story did not explain the picture on the milk carton or the dress that was in the trunk? *(page 94, during the night)* Why are problems always worse during the night? What descriptive words did the author use to describe Janie's brain and her thinking? *(page 94, "...an idea misted in her brain like fog: dank and sour and thick.")*

9. What new information did Janie get in her daymares? *(page 95, toddlers in high chairs pounding spoons, laughter ricocheting off the kitchen walls)* Do these images go with your ideas of a cult?

Prediction:
Why does Janie cut class and want Reeve to drive to New Jersey? What will she learn there?

Supplementary Activities:
1. What did Janie learn about Hannah? Make an attribute web for Hannah.

2. Art Activity: There aren't any illustrations in this novel. If you were an illustrator, what pictures would you add? Why? Use any type of media to make an illustration that you think would add to the novel. Write a paragraph explaining how this illustration would help the reader.

3. Literary Analysis—Cause/Effect: When one examines the reason for events in a story, we often find that: a) one cause has several results, or b) several causes lead to the same result. Begin Cause/Effect Charts for Janie, her parents, and Hannah. (See page 26 of this guide for an example.)

Cause/Effect Chart

Directions: When examining the reason for events in a story, we often find that:

a) one cause has several results, or
b) several causes lead to the same result.

1. Think about the various effects the kidnapping has on the families. Organize the chain of events it sets off within the map below.

   How do little Jennie's actions affect the Springs, Hannah, and the Johnsons?

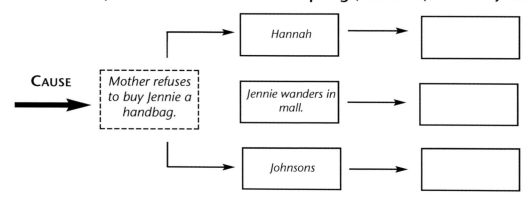

2. Organize some of these reasons (causes of actions) within the map below.

   Why does Jennie leave her mother?

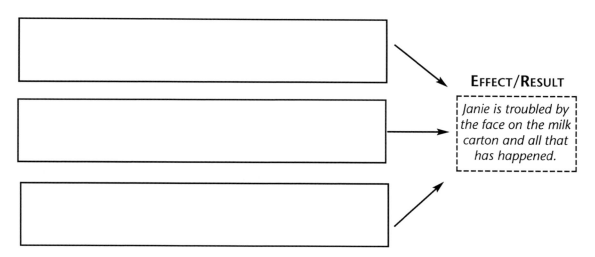

Chapter 11: Pages 100-114
Chapter 12: Pages 115-119

Vocabulary:

      conspiracy 101   time warp 103   leverage 112   preposterous 113

Vocabulary Activity:
Each student or cooperative group will make a poster, banner, or sign to advertise their word or words. The ad must show what the word means and how to pronounce it. The words will be displayed and should be signed by the artist(s).

Discussion Questions and Activities:
1. Although Janie filled Reeve in on the details about what she had discovered, why wasn't he comfortable about finding the Spring family from the milk carton? (page 102) Why was Reeve worried about his parents?

2. Why did Reeve tell Janie about all his problems growing up with his super-achiever brothers and sisters? (page 104)

3. What made Janie feel Reeve loved her? (page 106) What did Reeve think the Springs would do if Janie rang their doorbell? How could this affect Janie's parents? How would you answer Reeve's objections to ringing the Springs' doorbell?

4. What did Janie and Reeve learn when they drove by the Springs' house? *(Pages 110-112, Two red-haired boys, about sixth-graders, went into the house. The woman who opened the door had red hair too. A big high school boy with red hair also went into the house.)* How did this tie into Janie's daymares?

5. Although Reeve and Janie registered at a motel, they did not stay. Can you explain what made them change their minds? (page 116)

Prediction:
What will the parents do with Reeve and Janie? If you were the parents, how would you handle this situation?

Supplementary Activities:
1. Literary Analysis—Style: Just as people have certain hair styles or clothing styles, authors have particular styles of writing. An author's style depends on the words he or she uses and the types of sentences he or she writes. Some authors use many words that appeal to the senses or figures of speech. Other writers write in short sentences or use simple "spare" prose. How would you describe Cooney's writing style in *The Face on the Milk Carton*?

2. Role play the parents talking to their children.

3. Character Chart: Make a large character chart. Add characters as we meet them in the novel. For each of the characters, describe when they experience the feelings listed.

Feeling	Janie	Frank	Miranda	Reeve	Hannah
anger					
fear					
frustration					
relief					
happiness					
love					
pride					
insecurity					

Chapter 13: Pages 120-136
Chapter 14: Pages 137-146

Vocabulary:

taut 120	basked 121	pertly 128	peruse 129
plausible 130	invariably 133	access 135	flippant 138

Vocabulary Activity:
Put the vocabulary words in alphabetical order. Arrange the words in sets of two. Use each set of words in the same sentence.

Discussion Questions and Activities:
1. Why did Janie bask in her parents' anger? *(Pages 120-121, "They're my mother and father…That's why they're so mad. That's what mothers and fathers do.")* How did Reeve's parents' anger differ from Janie's, or did it? How was some of this anger resolved? *(Page 122, Janie said Reeve had helped her by talking to her.)*

2. What did Janie's parents think could have happened to Hannah? (pages 123-124) What did happen to the many young people who joined cults in the 1960s?

3. Why didn't Janie talk about what they saw in New Jersey? How would that have changed the direction of the story?

4. Why did Janie look up Jennie Springs in the *New York Times* even though she was determined never to let her parents know what was bothering her? What do you think Janie's parents would have done if they knew about New Jersey? What did Janie learn from the *New York Times*? *(Page 134, No ransom had been asked for Jennie.)* What might that indicate? Why didn't Janie look at the picture of the family which was in the paper?

5. How did Janie see pizza as a "buy off"? *(Page 138, Janie's mother usually served "solid" food, but she would give her "Anything–just don't leave the way Hannah did.")*

6. Why did the Johnsons want Reeve to go home and let them go out for pizza? *(Page 138, They wanted Janie to themselves and Janie's mother wanted to talk about getting family counseling.)* Do you think counseling would have helped the family? Why or why not? Why did Janie refuse counseling? *(Page 139, She was having a hard time with her lies to her friends and her family, and she knew it would be even harder to keep up her front with a psychiatrist who specialized in adolescent trauma.)*

7. What new fact came to Janie in her daymare? *(Page 139, "She, who lived in a household without religion, knew a prayer." Also, her real father wanted them to be quiet.)*

8. What did Janie try to write in her notebook? *(page 140, a letter to the Springs)* What interesting things did she try to tell them? How would the Springs feel if Janie really mailed them such a letter?

9. How did Janie blame herself? *(Page 144, She gave up a wonderful family for an ice cream sundae.)* Can she be sure that the Springs did not abuse her or were mean to her? *(Pages 144-145, Janie thought she was a rotten little kid who wanted more attention and was willing to be kidnapped to get it.)* Why did Janie in a way want to go to the Adolescent Trauma Center? *(page 145, to figure out why she didn't remember the Springs family sooner)*

10. Are most three-year-olds able to give their addresses and home phone numbers?

Prediction:
Will Janie ever put out of her mind the milk carton and the little dress in the trunk? How will Janie resolve her problems if she won't go to counseling, tell her parents about the milk carton, go to the police or the Springs?

Supplementary Activities:
1. Literary Analysis—Mood: When one feeling in a story is stronger than the others, that feeling is called the mood of the story. What is the mood at the end of Chapter 14? How does the author's description create that mood?

2. Review the chapters of this novel. For Janie, provide a phrase describing her emotions in each chapter. Complete the chart on page 31 of this guide. For example, in Chapter 1, Janie might have been completely stunned when she found her face on the milk carton. What does it mean to be on an "emotional roller coaster"? What range of emotions did Janie feel?

Chapter 15: Pages 147-157
Chapter 16: Pages 158-167

Vocabulary:
> innuendo 151   automaton 154   enveloped 159

Vocabulary Activity:
The students will use vocabulary words from this chapter, plus others of their choosing, to make crossword puzzles on graph paper. The students will write a question for each word and develop an answer sheet. The teacher will check the answers and distribute the puzzles to other students.

Discussion Questions and Activities:
1. Why did Janie think writing in her notebook was good? *(Page 147, "Writing cleansed: it removed the badness from her mind and kept it safely on the paper.")* Does writing really help with problems?

2. Why did Reeve tell his sister about the kidnapping? *(Page 153, Reeve thought Janie was losing her mind.)* Was this a good idea? Why or why not?

3. What ideas did Lizzie have? *(Pages 153-154, Lizzie thought that Hannah had kidnapped Janie, not Janie's parents.)* How did Lizzie determine who was the individual who had really done the kidnapping? *(Page 154, Janie's parents were good people who just would not kidnap. They would never have been part of anything criminal or evil.)* How did this thinking help Janie?

4. What problems did Lizzie foresee? *(Page 155, If they told anybody what they suspected, the FBI would be called in because kidnapping is a federal crime and they would have to locate Hannah.)*

Feelings

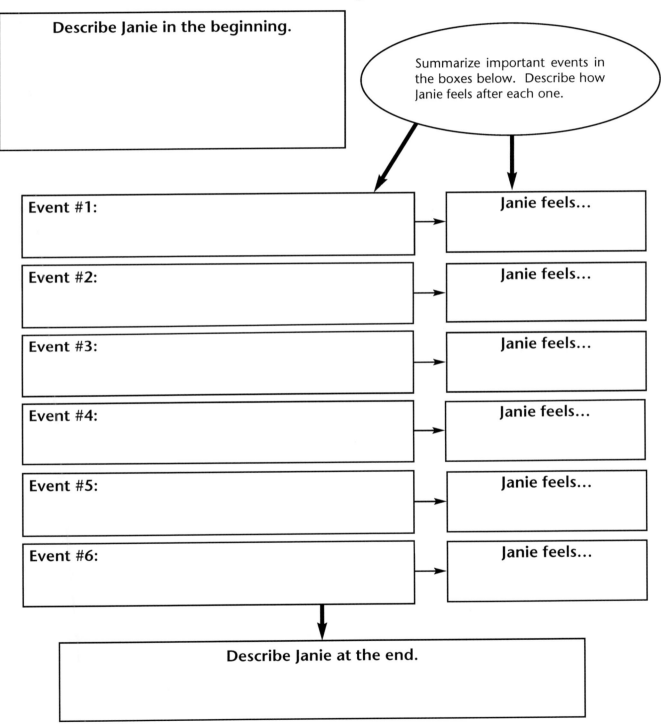

Describe Janie in the beginning.

Summarize important events in the boxes below. Describe how Janie feels after each one.

Event #1:

Janie feels...

Event #2:

Janie feels...

Event #3:

Janie feels...

Event #4:

Janie feels...

Event #5:

Janie feels...

Event #6:

Janie feels...

Describe Janie at the end.

5. Did Janie's friends know something was bothering her? *(Page 159, Yes. "You open your notebook twenty times a day and stare down into that milk carton.")* Did her mother know why she was upset when her notebook fell open? How could Janie have handled these situations without telling the truth? What would have happened if she had told the truth right then?

6. Why couldn't Janie destroy the milk carton? (page 159) What did Reeve mean when he called the milk carton "Pandora's box"? (page 161)

7. What were Janie's theories on why Frank and Miranda had not read about the kidnapping and seen her picture? *(Page 161, They were distracted by Janie and Hannah.)*

8. Why were Janie's friendships with Sarah-Charlotte and Reeve in trouble? *(Page 164-167, Janie was so troubled about her kidnapping and her past that she was no longer fun to be with.)*

Prediction:
What are Janie's options?

Chapter 17: Pages 168-175
Chapter 18: Pages 176-184

Vocabulary:

conspicuous 170	dawdling 171	anorexia 171	demented 174
audibly 175	haggard 178	grotesque 181	velocity 181

Vocabulary Activity:
Write at least three sentences using two or more vocabulary words in a sentence.

Discussion Questions and Activities:
1. What did Janie think really mattered to Reeve? *(Page 169, "Being first in somebody's life.")* Why had Reeve broken up with Janie? *(Page 169, She had put New Jersey first.)*

2. What did Janie plan to do with her letter to the Springs? *(Page 170, She would take the letter, the milk carton, and the polka-dot dress and put them back in the trunk in the attic. That was how she was going to handle the problem.)*

3. What really upset Janie about the Pity Party? *(Page 171, Sarah-Charlotte was going to invite a girl named Jodie. This triggered another daymare for Janie. She remembered that one of her sisters was named Jodie.)*

4. What triggered Janie to talk to Lizzie? *(Page 173, She had lost the addressed letter to the Springs.)*

5. Why did Reeve think Janie had lost the letter? *(Page 174, Reeve told Janie that it was no accident. "You had to get out of this somehow, and that's the route you took.")*

6. How do you think Janie told her parents the truth? (page 176) Why do you think the author did not include this important scene in the book?

7. Why didn't Janie want to meet the Springs? *(Page 181, "They aren't real right now. I don't want them to be real. I want them to go away.")* Was Janie realistic?

8. What did Lizzie mean when she said, "It'll never be over"? (page 182)

Prediction:
What will take place in the phone call to the Spring Family?

Postreading Questions and Activities

1. Are you satisfied with the ending of the novel? How else might the story have ended? Would a "happy" ending have been better? Why do you think Cooney chose this one? Do you want to read the sequel?

2. Theme is the novel's central idea. What is the author's message? Why do you think the author wrote this story? Support your ideas for theme or themes with examples from the novel. Is the central theme of this story presented directly or indirectly?

3. Characterization: Characters are developed by what they say, think, and do, and by how others in the novel react to them. Review the attribute webs. Which character in this story provided wisdom and perspective? How did the characters change during the story? How would you explain the changes?

4. Choose three events in the story, and write two or three paragraphs about how changing these events would have changed what happened in the story.

5. What most surprised you about this book? Write three sentences to answer these questions.

6. Write a set of questions which others reading the book should be able to answer. Write a set of answers. Compare your questions with a classmate.

7. Summarize the story using the story diagram below.

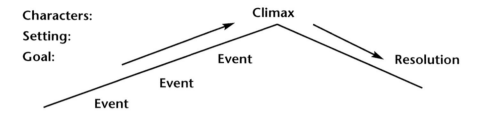

Characters:
Setting:
Goal:

Climax

Event

Resolution

Event

Event

8. Complete the Critical Thinking Sheet on page 37 of this guide.

Extension Activities

Writing:
1. Write a newspaper article for a New Jersey paper about the newly found kidnapped girl.

2. Write a letter from Janie to her parents (either set) after a year.

3. Write an essay in which you compare and contrast Janie before and after reading the milk carton. First, organize ideas with a Venn diagram. Include personality, attitude, abilities, etc.

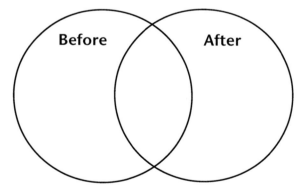

Before   After

4. Write a new ending for the story.

5. Make a list of predictions about what happened to Reeve and Janie after this story ended.

6. Complete the story pyramid on page 36 of this guide.

7. Write a poem that might have fallen out of Janie's notebook.

Listening/Speaking:
1. Retell an episode from a chapter from the viewpoint of Miranda or Frank.

2. Pretend you are a radio journalist. Interview Janie or Mrs. Spring about the ordeal of the kidnapping.

3. Role play/Interview: A panel of four students representing Janie, Hannah, Mrs. Spring, and Mrs. Johnson face the class, which has prepared a list of questions to ask the characters in the story. Each panel member wears something and/or carries a simple prop which characterizes the role that person is assuming.

Language Study:
1. Collect your favorite descriptions. How does the reader see and feel the scenes?

2. Figurative Language: A *metaphor* is a comparison between two things without the words "like" or "as." A *simile* is a comparison using the words "like" or "as." *Personification* is giving human characteristics to an animal or object. Find examples of metaphors, similes, and personification in the novel. Make these lists part of the bulletin board. Then create your own examples of figurative language.

Art:
1. Draw a picture of Janie at age three, and one at the time of the novel. On the back of the pictures, describe in words how she had changed.

2. What are the five major events in the novel? Draw five pictures to depict these events. Write captions for each drawing. This may be a cooperative group project or a class mural.

3. Make a collage about *The Face on the Milk Carton*. Include important symbols and words that summarize the story.

Story Pyramid

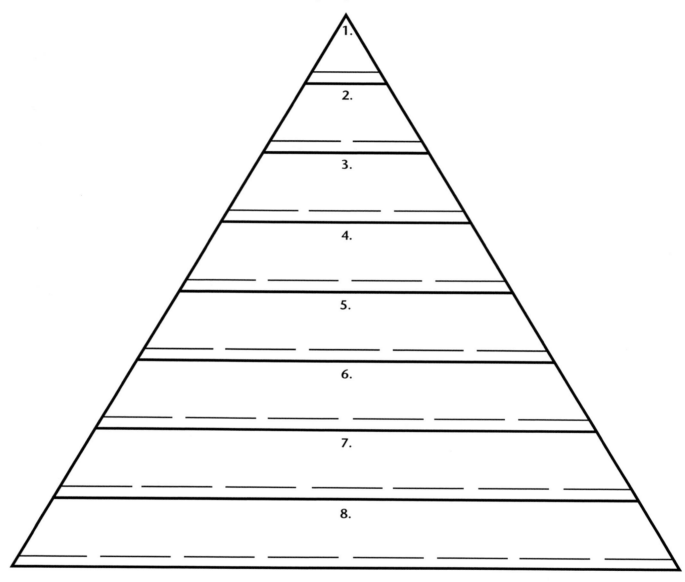

1. One word naming the main character.
2. Two words describing the main character.
3. Three words describing the setting.
4. Four words describing the problem.
5. Five words that represent the first main event.
6. Six words that represent the second main event.
7. Seven words for the third main event.
8. Eight words for the resolution of the story.

Critical Thinking Sheet

The Face on the Milk Carton was made into a made-for-TV movie, but at this time, it is not available on video.

Discuss how you would make the book *The Face on the Milk* Carton into a movie. Some questions to explore are:

1. In casting for the major roles, what physical and emotional qualities would you look for?

2. Where would you do the filming?

3. What music would you use for the soundtrack? Where would you have music play?

4. With what scene would you open the movie?

5. What scenes from the book would you leave out? Why?

6. What additional scenes not in the book would you add? Why?

7. With what scene would you end?

8. Would you change the ending of the book in the movie? How? Why?

9. Write a review of the movie for your school newspaper.

10. Write and produce a TV commercial promoting the movie.

Teacher Information

Kidnap:

Definition: to abduct or detain a person or animal, often for a ransom. A 1990 U.S. Justice Department study reports that more than 350,000 children are abducted each year by a family member (8 of 10 abductors are parents or parental figures) based on reported incidents. Around 75,000 suffer serious emotional, physical, or sexual abuse. Parental abductions are growing at an "alarming rate" according to Ernie Allen, president of the National Center for Missing and Exploited Children, a non-profit organization based in Arlington, Virginia.

Mass-mailing fliers like the ones put out by Hartford-based ADVO, inc. (elongated post cards with advertising on one side and missing children on the other) are considered nuisance mail to most people. They do, however remote, hold out the possibility that someone, somewhere, might recognize the children.

Cult:

Definition: a system or community of religious worship; a group that uses methods that deprive individuals of their ability to make a free choice. They use deceitful recruitment techniques, they deceptively and destructively use the devotee's energies, and they capture the devotee's mind.

ASSESSMENT FOR *THE FACE ON THE MILK CARTON*

Assessment is an on-going process, more than a quiz at the end of the book. Points may be added to show the level of achievement. When an item is completed, the teacher and the student check it.

Name _____ Date _____

Student   **Teacher**

_____   _____   1. On a piece of posterboard, develop a missing child poster for Jennie. Illustrate the poster with a picture of the child in the polka dot dress.

_____   _____   2. Complete attribute webs for Janie and her "parents."

_____   _____   3. Complete the "insecurity web" as a prewriting activity for a short paper on some insecurity that you have felt.

_____   _____   4. Choose one conflict in your life. Describe the conflict. Identify the type and describe how it was resolved.

_____   _____   5. There aren't any illustrations in this novel. If you were an illustrator, what pictures would you add? Why? Use any type of media to make an illustration that you think would add to the novel. Write a paragraph explaining how this illustration would help the reader.

_____   _____   6. Write a letter from Janie to her parents (either set) after a year.

_____   _____   7. Use the *Readers' Guide to Periodical Literature* in the library to locate articles about real-life kidnappings. Read one of the true-life stories you find, and write a comparison and contrast to the story of Janie.

_____   _____   8. Give yourself one point for each vocabulary activity completed.

_____   _____   9. Write a poem about something in this novel. You may use the story pyramid or any poetic form that you wish.

_____   _____   10. Pantomime a scene from the story and see if classmates can figure out which scene it is.

Notes